The Pipers' Guild Handbook

By
Margaret James

This Handbook was first published in 1932, revised by the Author in May, 1947, and dedicated, as before,
to
HILDA M. KING
Head Mistress of Finlay Street School, Fulham, London, England where the first pipes were made in 1926.

Copyright © 2013 Read Books Ltd.
This book is copyright and may not be
reproduced or copied in any way without
the express permission of the publisher in writing

British Library Cataloguing-in-Publication Data
A catalogue record for this book is available from the
British Library

A Short History of Musical Notation

Musical Notation is any system used to visually represent aurally perceived music through the use of written symbols – including ancient or modern musical symbols. Although many ancient cultures used symbols to represent melodies, none of these systems are nearly as comprehensive as written language, limiting knowledge of ancient music to a few fragments. Although it has incredibly old roots, comprehensive music notation only began to be developed in Europe in the **Middle Ages** but has since been adapted to many kinds of music worldwide.

The earliest form of musical notation can be found in a cuneiform tablet that was created at Nippur, in today's Iraq around 2000 BC. The tablet represents fragmentary instructions for performing music, that the music was composed in harmonies of thirds, and that it was written in a diatonic scale. A tablet from about 1250 BC shows a more developed form of notation, and though the interpretation of the system is still controversial, it is clear that the notation indicates the names of strings on a lyre. Although fragmentary, these tablets represent the earliest notated melodies found anywhere in the world.

The ancient Greeks used musical notation from at least the sixth century BC until approximately the fourth century AD, and several complete compositions and fragments using this notation survive. This system consisted of symbols placed above text syllables, and the Delphic Hyms, dated to the second century BC use this notation – but are not completely preserved. Such methods appear to have fallen out of use around the time of the Decline of the Roman Empire. The Byzantine Empire was the other major civilisation to use musical notation, and theirs was remarkably similar to subsequent Western notation, in that it was ordered left to right, and separated into measures. The main difference is that the Byzantine notation symbols were *differential* rather than absolute, i.e. they indicate pitch *change* (rise or fall), and the musician had to deduce correctly, from the score and the note they were singing, which note came next.

In early Europe, a rough form of notation for remembering Gregorian chants was established, but the problem with this system was that it only showed melodic contours – and consequently the music could not be read by someone who did not know the tune. To address the issue of exact pitch, a staff was introduced consisting originally of a single horizontal line, but this was progressively extended until a system of four parallel, horizontal lines was standardized. This is traditionally attributed to **Guido of Arezzo**, who set out his thoughts on the changes in his first musical treatise, *Micrologus* (1026). The modern five-line staff was first adopted in France and became almost universal by the sixteenth century (although the use of staves with other numbers of lines was still widespread well into the seventeenth century).

As is evident from this incredibly short and potted history, musical notation has differed vastly over time – but has been adopted all over the globe. The modern musical notation we use today originated in European classical music, but is now used by musicians of many different genres throughout the world. The system, like that developed in France uses a five-line staff, and pitch is shown by placement of **notes** on the staff (sometimes modified by **accidentals**), and duration is shown with different **note values** and additional symbols such as **dots** and **ties**. There are also some specialised notation conventions, for example for percussion instruments or chord charts which contain little or no melodic information at all but provide detailed harmonic and rhythmic information, using slash notation and rhythmic notation. This is the most common kind of written music used by professional session musicians playing **jazz** or other forms of **popular music** and is intended primarily for the **rhythm section** (usually containing **piano**, **guitar**, **bass** and **drums**). We hope the reader is inspired by this book to find out more about this fascinating subject.

CHAPTER I.

The Story of Pipe-Making.

A poor man may buy a bamboo stick for a few pence and carve it with a pocket knife into the shape of a flute. What kind of music can he expect to conjure out of anything so easily acquired? Real music? Impossible!

This little book, however, is written to prove the excellence of such music.

In these days when we expect to pay heavily in money and in years of labour for everything that is good, pipe-making is an exception and a surprise.

It is time to restore an active share in music to everyone, not only to the musician but to the worker, whatever his trade may be. At present, his share is merely passive. He is pushed out of the realm of creative music and told to listen to the more fortunate specialist. He is, in fact, to appreciate the music of a few professionals instead of his own. This is difficult, because spontaneous and intelligent appreciation comes from our practical knowledge of a subject: from our power to do the thing ourselves. This is the sane and healthy way of appreciation and since it is denied to us, we have tried to fill the gap with broadcast discussions on technicalities or with sermons on musical construction, These are fun for the lecturer, for he is expressing what is dear to him through personal experience. To the listener they are mere shadow of substance: until he has proved these things by his own creative music-making he is not in a position to enjoy them.

We are so dependent on machinery that we forget the use of our own hands, so accustomed to pay a heavy price for what we value that we ignore the use of simple materials. In pipe-making our hands are used to fashion a perfectly common piece of wood and the result is a treasure. Having recovered from our surprise we assimilate the principle. The pipe is a gift from nature: had it been purchased at the music shop for twenty pounds, its value would have been less, not more.

While we make our pipes they bring us into touch with nature's magic in conjuring a note from a hollow piece of wood; with her dainty requirements and the way her science works. She gives us, meanwhile, music of a very rare and beautiful kind, precisely in tune if we will have it so, and mellow in tone.

The secret of pipe music has always belonged to the European peasant. On the Albanian hills, in Sicily, Armenia and Russia, or further afield still, in India, shepherds and goat-herds carve cane and reed with a knife, and find a mellow tone in the hollow of its stalk. All that is left for us to do is a careful adaptation of his craft, and a readjustment of his scale, which

Copyright MCMXXXII for all countries by J. B. Cramer & Co. Ltd.   J.B.C. & Co., Ltd. 13084 he makes in random pitch, so that we may play English melodies in the civilised musical convention. When the adaptation is complete, we have something which unites handicraft and design with music, so that we can understand and enjoy all three.

Having spent less than five shillings on tools, we make any number of pipes inexpensively. The beauty of tone, and the great number of ways in which pipe music may be used, turn the adventure into true musical education. This we must prove for ourselves by following the directions to be given presently.

In 1926 experiments were tried in a Fulham school with little shop-made pipes. When these failed by reason of their uncertain pitch and the shortness of their lives, the pipe of a Sicilian goatherd was found in a drawer, laid by and dusty for lack of use : a mere curiosity. It had been carved by the goatherd in his native country, some years previously. Sitting by the roadside, he whittled a bundle of cane with his knife (his speed incredible, I am told) and sold the results to passers by. A pipe fell into the hands of a sympathetic traveller from England, who bought it, and sent it by post to me. It was a length of white bamboo with a loud mellow voice, a wooden mouthpiece, fipple head and a scale of holes round which a carved pattern meandered. The re-discovery of this "flageolet" happened in summer time, and English bamboo pipes were made in a Cotswold garden, very roughly hewn from a length of cane found in the tool shed. They were an attempt to imitate the work of the Sicilian peasant, but when they were finished, the only promise of success they gave was a hoarse, gruff note. Their narrow bore made anything else impossible, but the sound represented some kind of pitch, and the mere discovery was an adventure. Instead of the wooden mouthpiece, a cork was pushed into the hollow tube ; this was meant for experimental purposes, but its use was such a success, that it has become permanent.

The second expedition was no longer to a tool shed but to an attic, where, amid even more dust, there lay a bamboo curtain pole. Artificially mottled and varnished in the fashion of fifty years ago, closed each end with a demure brass ornament, it had seen its day, and had been laid to rest. However, the ornaments were sawn off, and, to the surprise of the household, this curtain rod, divided into lengths, was persuaded to yield limpid scales in different keys, which at least rivalled those made by the goatherd. The pipes were enamelled in brilliant colours and were carried back to Fulham long before they were dry. The reception they met from the boys and girls there was rapturous, and they were blown by all to the detriment of their decoration.

The possibility of pipe-making was already proved beyond a doubt, and a group of jolly boys began to learn the craft and to make experiments in it themselves.

The sympathy and discrimination of the Headmistress in the school enabled us to work during school hours, with a group admirably chosen for the purpose. The boys, about eight in number, were not selected for musical talent; they had different qualifications for the class. Two were unmusical boys, chosen for their love of handicraft and painting, two were scientific and intelligent without special artistic ability, and the others came primarily for love of music.

In spite of all the early mistakes in our pipe-making, the instruments that failed, the difficulties in tuning and the cracks, we discovered many of nature's secrets, and formed our little orchestra. The boys who cared most to use their hands found that in doing so they were making music, and a new interest in melody dawned upon them. Laboriously at first, they achieved a single tune, and this opened the way for more. They joined the band with new delight. The scientific boys made experiments in sound which delighted them, and which awakened their interest in music as a whole. Musical boys loved to learn to use their hands in such a cause, and for all, the delight of painting came to reward their work. The interdependence of handwork, design and music was shown to be the main thought underlying the whole experiment, even in this early, stumbling class. It is still the inspiration of every pipe band. The achievement is threefold, and each aspect of it brings understanding to the whole. The first pipe band, composed of fifteen boys and girls in procession, played carol melodies as they slowly descended from a staircase into a darkened room, other children escorting them with coloured lanterns. This happened during the Christmas season following the summer of 1926, when the first pipes were made. The effect of the combined piping was gentle and beautiful, admirably suited to the tune they played " I Saw Three Ships Come Sailing By."

Afterwards, pipes of various kinds were tried and added to the orchestra, efforts, mostly unsuccessful, being made to blend them. Transverse alto and tenor flutes were all found to have their special beauty and value, but the way to perfect and combine them was not discovered until some years later. Meanwhile, the first pipes were in a constant state of experiment and improvement, and the head, especially the mouth or " window," as it was called, passed through various sizes and shapes from season to season. It was considered " old-fashioned " to play tunes with a window that was " out of date "; indeed, I heard one boy describing another's pipe as " Elizabethan "!. The children felt that musical possibilities were growing fast, and knew the joy of playing in parts. Country dances, classical songs and rounds were tackled successfully. On one occasion the orchestra played for country dancing; on another a group of twelve chosen pipers played " Summer is icumen in " in four parts.

The Christmas band of 1927 was increased in size to the number of about eighty children, all the makers of the pipes they played. The volume of soft, clear tone was beautiful, but many difficulties had become apparent by this time, and the instruments were not exactly in tune, especially on the night of their performance.

It was now obvious that the band had grown too quickly and had come into being before each member of it had grasped the essentials. On warm days and in stuffy rooms, pipes became out of tune, and their readjustment, especially in such large numbers, became an overwhelming task. It was not until much later, and after unhurried work in remote places, that the essentials could be formulated for making a truly successful pipe band. It was found that the number of players must grow by degrees, after a solid musical nucleus had been established. Like all music and art, in or out of school, beauty comes surely, but gradually, after time and perseverance. Tuning difficulties have been solved with tiny pieces of matchstick and elastic, which give to each pipe a sliding scale. We have partly learned, too, the art of blending instruments of different sorts, and the place and value of a pianoforte accompaniment.

This knowledge came later, when Fulham had been left behind. In a tiny village school, consisting of twenty-three children who lived in a steep Cotswold Valley, seventeen boys and girls learned to make pipes of every kind, and to play them seriously and tunefully. At first they were embarrassed with the strangeness of the undertaking, deaf to pitch and slow to perceive or to understand any form of music. Melody crept slowly into their consciousness as they discovered the art of making it, and the joy of pipes dawned upon them finally, when they found themselves painting with a brush, in bright, clear colours. By degrees every detail, from the first cut of the saw to the final playing in parts, had its appeal for them. Enthusiasm came, of a solid, lasting kind, and with the enthusiasm a power to detect the slightest falsity or variation in pitch, a power to appreciate melody and rhythm and, finally, a love of composing it themselves. With little or no help several made their own melodies at home, wrote them in numbers or notes on a stave of five lines and came back to the band to play them. We tried many experiments and learned to be as philosophical over failure as we were overjoyed with success.

All this was a matter of more than two years. By that time the little ones, taught by elder brothers and sisters, had learned to play at home by the kitchen fire. The process must have been one of immense patience on the part of the teachers and immense and plodding keenness on the part of the pupils, for the younger aspirants were seldom more than seven years old. When they were ready, playing a slow melody with painstaking accuracy, their proud elders introduced them to the band. This work was a mutual arrangement on the part of the children, without any suggestion given at school.

One boy musician of eleven played at home every morning as soon as he was awake upon pipe, piccolo or flute, and himself made a flute of his own bicycle pump, sacrificed to music, and quite successfully so. In another home, a little girl aged eight, herself quite new to the band, plodded patiently with the tuition of " Dinah," aged six, a person with pluck, aspiration and yellow curls. When the pipers met for the first time after the Christmas holidays, the elder sister volunteered her report of progress. " Dinah can play ' Twinkle, Twinkle Little Star ' now, but she squeaks." Still, there was never any doubt of the final success ; Dinah was in the band before March. Finally, a little boy who was mentally backward, and who resented the huge effort to master his fingers with his brain, finally conquered this, and then played in an exact, deliberate style. The other children, watching his progress, summed up the situation by saying " He's got as 'e likes it !"

It speaks well for the gentle tone of the pipes that I never received a single complaint from the parents. Their quiet sympathy and encouragement were very helpful.

It is natural that other people should wish to share in our pleasure. As the demand grows the most natural reply to it seems to be an exact description of the way to make pipes, together with a short account of the musical use to which we have put them in the course of the experiment so far. We are still only at the beginning of the adventure which may develop in many ways, both in handcraft, decoration and musical achievement. The pipes, first started as an adventure in education for children, have become a means of music-making for grown-up people. Experience of teachers' classes proves this. Individuals of all ages from seven to seventy have made and played pipes with equal keenness and profit. Teachers often forget the ultimate aim in their schools as they find an absorbing pleasure and hobby for themselves. This is so because the instruments, far from being in any sense of the word "toys," are found to be something so original and beautiful in tone, so entrancing to use, that the handicraft leads to an intrinsically valuable possession. More than this, the primitive bamboo pipe lasts for ever, and improves like a violin or old wine, in the course of years. Families can make music in a way lost to us during the last two centuries, and this at the cost of a few shillings. Social workers can find a means of giving happiness to many groups of people of all ages, even if the beauty of the advanced orchestra is not always feasible. Everyone who makes a pipe will realise the significance of tone and pitch in a simple, direct way which contains its own pleasure.

Another thought follows naturally. **The players should make their own pipes ;** they should not buy them ready-made The demand has come from several places for bamboo pipes sold in numbers to provide an orchestra. The excuse for this is limitation of time.

The playing of a pipe is a small fraction of the good we can give to ourselves or to others. In a ready-made pipe band the knowledge of " how music comes " is lost, so is the ability to use our hands, the joy and achievement of making something which serves so beautiful a purpose, and the further joy of colour and decoration. Much of the education and happiness of the pipe band consists in the interdependence of the arts described earlier in this chapter, by means of which we gain understanding of each one by learning the rest. No one can deny that schooltime is short. Yet, how often the handwork and art produced during the long hours devoted to them are rather purposeless. How much better to surrender a few of our handwork hours to the service of design and music too. If, by our handwork, we make ourselves into musical human beings, can we say that the handwork itself loses in value? Surely it has increased in usefulness, losing nothing. Again, why invent designs on a sheet of paper during an art class, when we may allow our colours and patterns to decorate something which we shall use for ever in the service of music? Art teachers demand that design shall have a function; here is one which is great and useful beyond all expectation.

When the music, craft and art teachers are determined to combine their efforts to bring about a hand-made orchestra, there will be creative music in schools. Its quality will be beautiful beyond any expectation, and boys and girls will for ever after demand perfection of tone and pitch. When they leave school they will perfect handicraft, decoration and music-making in family life and in grown-up hand-made orchestras. The voices of pipes, played in three, four and five parts have a fine quality and can be very beautiful. Madrigals can be rendered with a subtlety of expression and phrasing which is peculiar to pipe music. We may go on, exploring new country step by step and finding new adventures with the increase of craftsmanship and musical understanding. In its perfected form pipe-making and playing is essentially an art for grown-up people.

How shall we begin? The directions given in the next chapter will teach us to make our pipes. While the scale is developing under our fingers we shall learn to manipulate the instrument, breathing gently and controlling our fingers to cover the notes as they appear.

Written directions, however, are only a preliminary step. Pipe making requires long practice and training before it can be mastered. No one should pass on his knowledge to a class until he has received personal training from a qualified Teacher of the Pipers' Guild, nor, if possible, before he has passed his own examination. For, although the first venture is open to all as a surprise and delight, it must lead us on to real study, knowledge of the craft, of technique and musicianship, without which the pipes degenerate into musical toys and are valueless.

CHAPTER II.

HOW TO MAKE A TREBLE PIPE.

MATERIALS AND TOOLS.

MATERIALS.

BAMBOO POLES (where possible). The poles chosen, except for tenor, should have thin walls, and should be uncracked. A six foot pole can be used to make five treble pipes in the key of D.

Diameter of Bore (inside measurement) :—
(a) For a treble pipe in D or C, $\frac{3}{4}$ to $\frac{7}{8}$ inch.
(b) For an alto pipe in A, $\frac{7}{8}$ to 1 inch.
(c) For a tenor, $1\frac{1}{4}$ inches or more.

2. CORKS.—These are chosen to fit the bamboo tightly when they are pushed in.

(*See J. B. Cramer's Pipe List for prices and full particulars*).

NECESSARY TOOLS.

1 PENKNIFE
2 RIMER BIT
3 WOODFILE
4 AUGER
5 HACKSAW

(1) A small sharp penknife.
(2) A foursquare rimer bit or with handle.
(3) A small flat ward file.
(4) An auger (half-inch size) for removing the joints of the bamboo. One is required for each orchestra. An individual pipe-maker, working at home, may substitute a red-hot poker.
(5) A medium-sized hacksaw, or small saw with small teeth.
Other tools may be added.
Price List on application.

Bamboo is at present in short supply. Applications should be made to the Pipers' Guild, which will keep in touch with all possible sources. Other Tubes and Corks (in all sizes) and necessary Tools for Pipe Making may be purchased at Messrs. Cramer & Co., Ltd., 139, New Bond Street, London, W.1. England.

All materials and tools are specially selected and approved, and are obtainable at small cost.

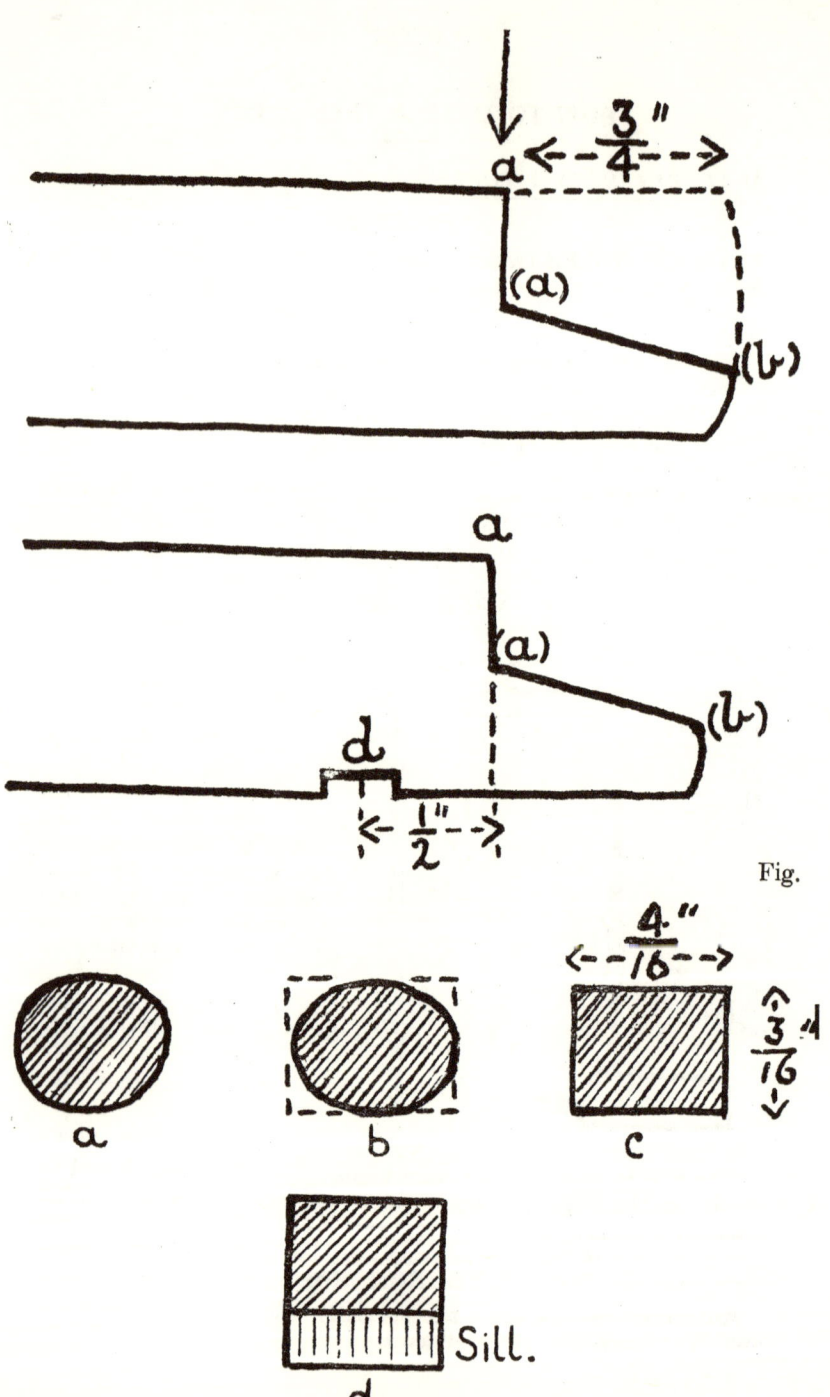

Fig.

Fig.

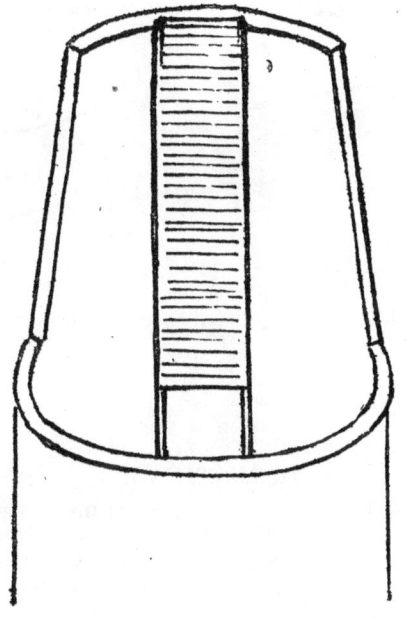

Fig. 3

4. Cork Cutting

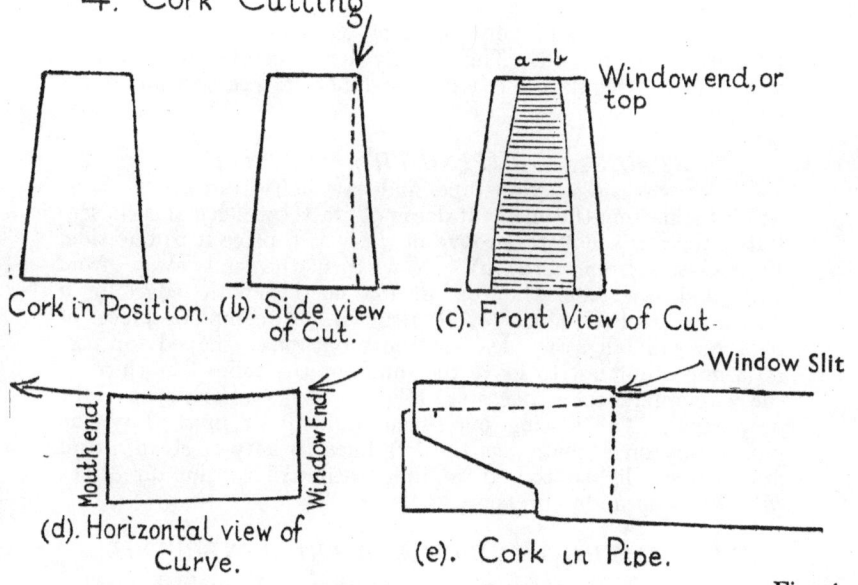

(b). Side view of Cut.

Cork in Position.

(c). Front View of Cut.

a—b Window end, or top

(d). Horizontal view of Curve.

Mouth end

Window End

(e). Cork in Pipe.

Window Slit

Fig. 4

5. Faulty Corks.

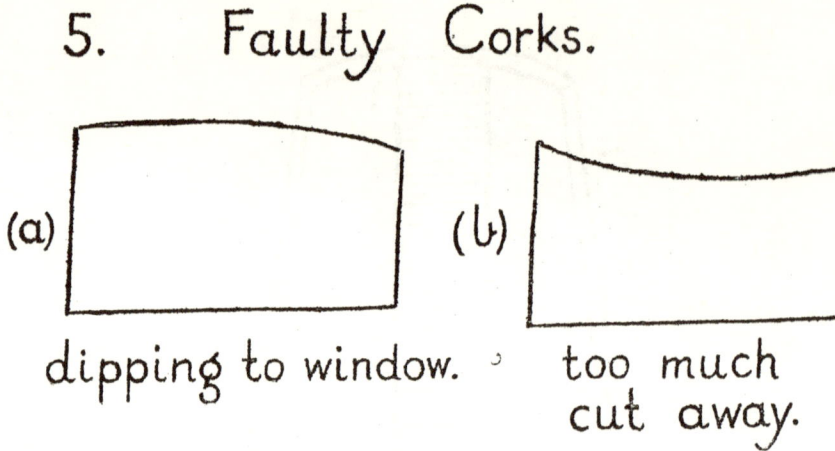

(a) dipping to window.   (b) too much cut away.

DIRECTIONS.

From the bamboo pole saw a piece to make your pipe. The length required is 11 in., and it will probably include a joint, which should be in the centre or thereabouts. Opinions differ as to the best position for a joint. The one *essential* is to have the mouthpiece end clear of joints for a distance of at least two inches from the end.

Now use an auger or red-hot poker to bore through the joint where it is solid, and your piece of bamboo becomes a hollow pipe from end to end. This is only a matter of a few seconds, and a little irregularity left on the inner surface will not affect the tone.

STAGE 1.—SHAPING THE MOUTHPIECE.

Take one end of your pipe, and saw halfway through it at a point ¾ in. from the end. It does not matter which end is chosen, but if there is a natural groove in the wood, place it to one side. Fig. 1—saw from *a* to (*a*). Now turn the end away from you, and saw from the top at (*b*), cutting both edges in a slanting direction until (*a*) is reached. A complete piece of bamboo will fall away, leaving the mouthpiece shaped for use. It is important not to leave too much at the top. One-third of the circumference is necessary Fig. 3 shows clearly the right proportion. The sawing may seem difficult at first. Lay the pipe firmly on a chair, use the left knee to keep it steady, and draw the saw lightly to and fro, in a downward slanting direction, without using undue pressure.

STAGE 2.—THE WINDOW AND THE WINDOW-SILL.

Now, at the point marked *d*, which is half an inch farther along than the first saw cut, but on the other side of the pipe, begin to bore a little hole with the point of your knife, holding the blade firmly between finger and thumb, and twisting it gently from side to side. By degrees the wood will be pierced. Then take a rimer and twist it steadily in the hole, using gentle pressure, until you have made a round opening three-sixteenths of an inch in diameter. Proceed carefully, for too large an opening will mean rough tone (Fig. 2a).

Now the hole must be squared and shaped. To do this, cut away the sides very slightly until it is just oval in shape (Fig. 2b). Finally, cut tiny V-shaped wedges from each corner with the point of a knife, and finish with a file. The window will be three-sixteenths of an inch high and four-sixteenths broad when it is finished, and neatly squared (Fig. 2c). Lack of care in the measurements, either of actual size or of placing, may affect the pipe's tone. It is easy to make too large and especially too deep a window, i.e. too long vertically, and this results in a husky tone. Use only the extreme point of the knife for making the window. In this way pressure may be applied without causing a crack.

The window-sill comes next. It is made by shaving the bottom edge of c until it slopes back at an angle of 45 degrees. The inner side is not cut away, but remains as an edge. This edge should be made nearly (but not quite) sharp to intercept the breath from the mouthpiece. The inside measurements of the window are not affected by its sill. It is most easily made by turning the pipe on its side, facing to the right, and using the desk or table as a support. Then small shavings may be cut away with the point of a knife. Finally the sill is neatly squared to the breadth of the window (Fig. 2d).

STAGE 3.—THE PASSAGE ROOF.

The passage roof is a shallow channel made on the inner side of the bamboo pipe. It runs from the window to the end of the mouthpiece (i.e. from d to b in Fig. 1). It is one-twentieth of an inch in depth, and is squared at the sides, not basin or wedge-shaped. Smooth and straight from side to side, exactly the same width as the window, it must not be humpy or irregular at any point, and should be finished with a file (Fig. 3). Although passage-making seems a difficult task at first, practice soon makes it easy.

STAGE 4.—THE CORK.

Choose a cork which will fit tightly, and which can be pushed into the mouthpiece until it is level with the top of the window The smaller end of the cork, which goes in first, should be an exact fit. If it is good, a slit appears between the cork and the passage roof at this point. It may be called the window slit. Blow gently into the mouthpiece, and your first note comes. This is simply a preliminary experiment in sound; sometimes it succeeds in producing a clear tone, sometimes not. In any case, the note may be brought to life or the tone improved by opening, slightly, the passage along which we blow. This is done by withdrawing the cork and cutting or filing from it a narrow shaving on the side which will later form the passage floor.

This shaving is cut in the following way :—hold the cork upright upon a firm surface, with the tapering end upwards and the side selected for cutting turned to the right. Cut from the top (see arrow in Fig. 4b), removing scarcely any surface at all as you begin, but directing the knife slightly inwards so that rather more is cut away as you proceed towards the thicker base. Use the knife as if it were a saw, applying little pressure. The face should be quite smooth, finished carefully with a file, should proceed from end to end without a hump, and must never dip downwards at the window. The *width* of the cut at the top or window end [see diagram 4c, a - - b] should be as nearly as possible the width of the window itself, i.e. $\frac{4}{16}$ ins. The drawings show the position of the cork when it is inserted and the appearance of the cut side of the cork.

Examine the cut corks in Fig. 5. The slightest tendency to these faults—here exaggerated for the sake of clearness—may be the cause of failure.

The tone of every pipe should be clear and mellow, although it will be found to vary in kind, according to the quality and shape of the bamboo. The following may be helpful to remember when you are fitting a cork :—**Tone depends mainly on the size of the window slit, through which the air is blown.** This is the space between the cork and bamboo as it appears at the point where the air emerges. Look into the top of the window from outside and you will see it. If it is barely visible, the note will be faint, and difficult to blow, and the higher octave more easily sounded than the lower or key note. As the slit is enlarged by filing the cork, the note increases in clearness and volume. This continues up to a point, but when the opening gapes too widely there is roughness, with a woody, husky quality. A very deep slit at the window will silence the note altogether. On the other hand at (*b*) in Fig. 1 there should be plenty of open space. In addition, the note depends on the Arch of the Sill. To see this is most important. Hold the pipe 18 inches or so *away from you*, slanting downwards so that light strikes the window from outside and look down the passage as in Fig. 6. Can you now see a little dark line of space, barely arched, below the window sill? This is the interior of the pipe beyond the window. The floor should always be low enough to admit of this being seen, but if too much has been cut away, it is large and the tone

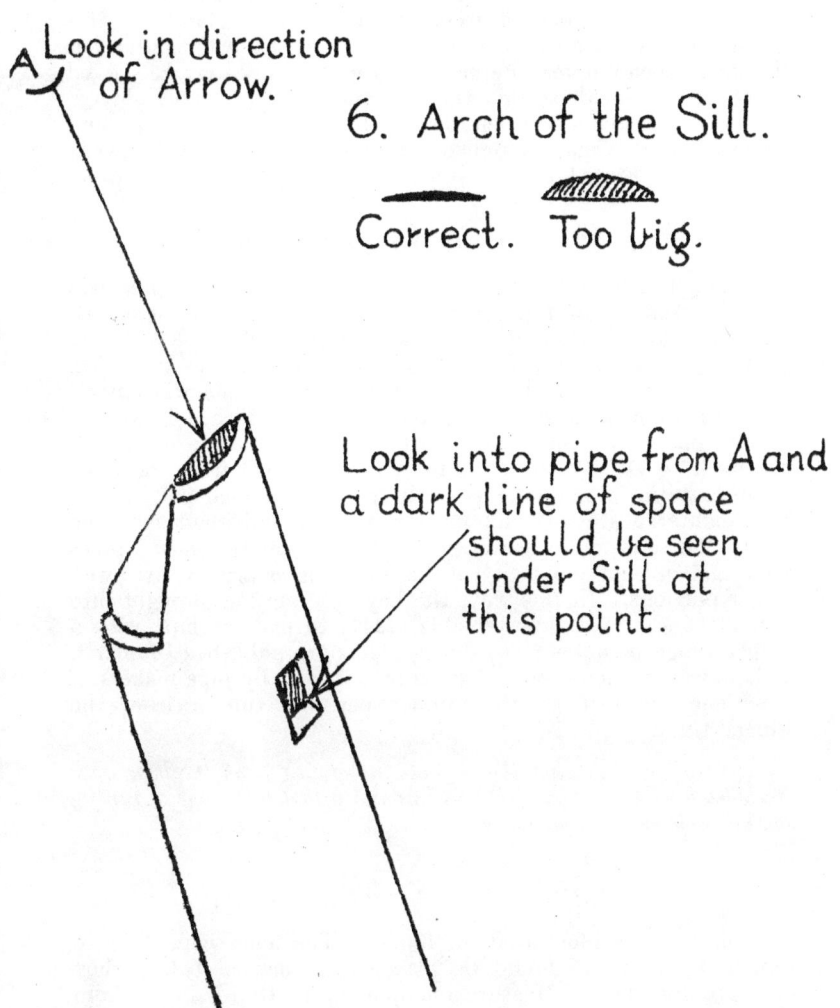

Fig. 6

is rough. A gaping space at this point will silence the pipe altogether. In the summary which I will give later on, this line of space is called " the arch of the sill."

Every pipe should sound at least two notes when its cork has been fitted, the key-note being produced by soft breathing and its harmonic octave when we blow rather harder. This second note need not be in tune; what we have to consider is the lower or key-note. Before we do so, the cork may be shaved away on the outside so that the pipe may be comfortably played. It is wise to leave a sufficient surface to be grasped by finger and thumb so that it may be pulled out as occasion requires [between (*a*) and (*b*) in Fig. 1]

STAGE 5.—TUNING THE KEY-NOTE.

The pitch we require for the key-note is D. Our pipe will probably sound lower than this. Take it to a piano, strike D, and then blow, softly and steadily. The pitch of a pipe is simply a matter of its length; the longer it is, the deeper its voice, and vice versa. For the length of a treble, a tone will correspond to an inch, and a semi-tone to half an inch. Therefore, if your pipe note is saying C, shorten the pipe by one inch. thus raising it to D. This is done by sawing an inch from the base. If at first the pipe's note is C sharp, half an inch will suffice. For slighter degrees of difference your own judgment must be used. These inside measurements given are safe to follow; pipes vary and in many cases it will be found necessary to saw away larger portions. In this way, the key-note may be brought into perfect tune. It is now possible (1947) to make a pipe with a longer range of notes (see New Scale Chart, published Cramers). This however, should not be attempted except by pipe makers of experience, and if possible, under personal tuition from the Pipers' Guild.

It is difficult to alter the keynote by sawing from the base once the holes have been made, so it is important that this stage of tuning should come in its right place.

STAGE 6.—MAKING THE HOLES.

This stage is illustrated in Fig. 7. The holes which are to represent the scale should be placed and marked before they are actually made. Measure one-quarter of the distance from the base of the pipe to the centre of the window; here mark the first hole. Then measure and mark $2\frac{1}{4}$ in. from the centre of the window. The six holes on the face of the pipe may be measured at equal distances between these two marks, the first and last marks representing the first and sixth holes respectively, and the other four being spaced between them. The holes should be about $\frac{7}{8}$ in. apart from centre to centre, but if you find that in so measuring them they exceed the limits provided by the first two marks, make them slightly nearer together. If the reverse occurs, and they do not reach the upper point, make a short gap between the first three and the last three, thus bridging the space.

In any case, the first hole should be carved exactly on the quarter mark, which should be most carefully measured, although the rule of thumb may suffice later on when you become an expert pipe-maker.

Now twist the point of a square awl (or knife) on the lowest mark, turning it from side to side, until a tiny hole pierces the bamboo. After this, insert a rimer bit or file end, and enlarge the hole by turning the rimer with gentle pressure. Do not allow it to remain in one position : it is a tool for making a round hole, and this by means of twisting. Pressure without twisting will cause a crack in the bamboo.

While the first hole is still small, blow your pipe, and you will find that its note has risen slightly. Enlarge it by degrees, blowing over and over again as the size increases, and the note ascends, until it gives you exactly the second note of the scale. If the pipe is in key D, this note should, of course, be E, and it may be tested by comparison with E on the piano or a pitch pipe. Close the hole firmly and once more the pipe returns to D.

By making another hole on the second point, you will find the third note of the scale, both holes now being left open. This must be enlarged until it is exactly in tune with F sharp, and **it will always be the largest hole of the series.**

The third opening, which gives G, represents a semi-tone and care should be taken not to make it too large.

The other notes follow, one by one, each being carefully pitched as it is opened. The scale must be made in this order, ascending step by step from the lowest note to the highest, for in no other way can a pipe be tuned. No measurement can be followed for the size of the holes, for they vary considerably every time a pipe is made, and the only guide we may trust is the ear. A thumb hole is added, to give the eighth or octave note, and this is placed just above and behind the sixth finger hole, on the other side of the pipe.

To tune a pipe well is a matter of practice. The usual difficulty comes when we reach the last four holes, the notes of which are found to be flat when the whole scale is played. This fault comes through blowing that is too forced, while we are making these holes. Each note must sound perfectly in tune when we ascend, beginning from D, and this with a soft, even breathing, that is no more violent as we reach the second half of the scale.

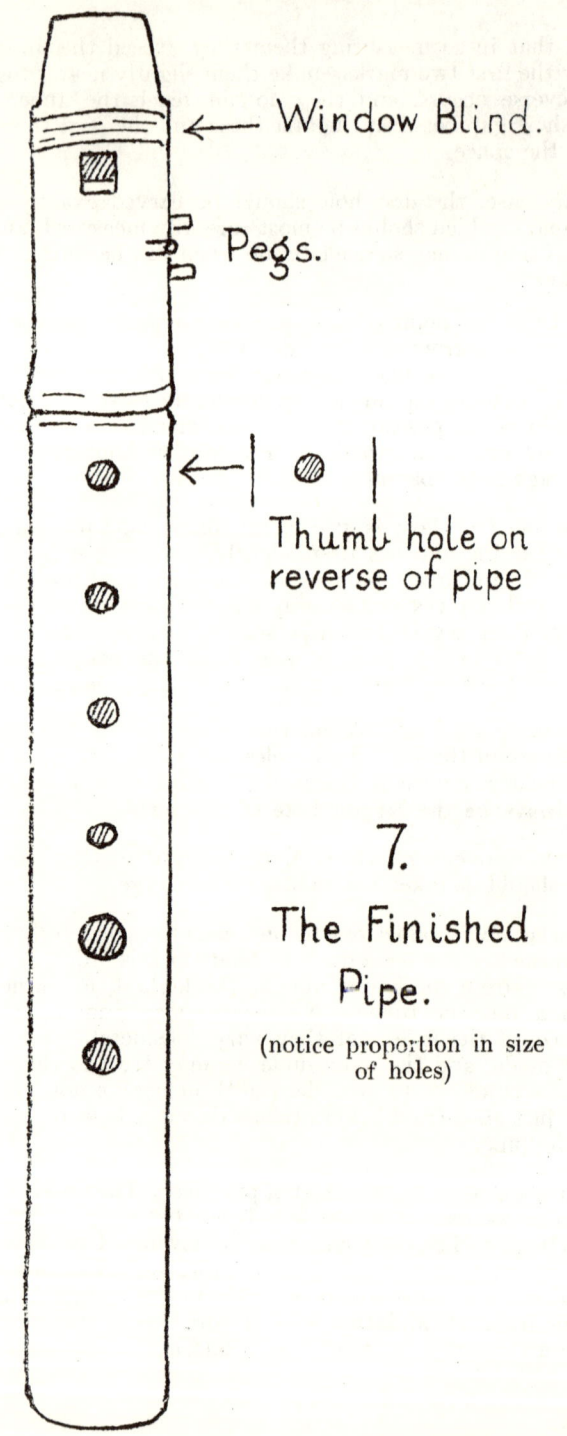

7.

The Finished Pipe.

(notice proportion in size of holes)

Making Pipes and Viols at Edgeworth, in the Cotswold Country.

It is wise to compare each note that is made with its equivalent on a piano. Another excellent test is to sing the intervals and then to play them. This applies to each step of the scale and to the intervals of the common chord when these become available. Remember that good tuning is absolutely essential.

When the pipe is finished, sound the intervals softly :—doh-me-so-doh.

CHAPTER III.

The Treble Pipe (*continued*).

THE pipe is now complete, but it will be subject to change from time to time, according to climate and circumstances. We must add something which will give us a sliding scale that we can adapt to different bands, piano, and seasons. Procure a small square awl with a sharp point. With this instrument bore a hole on the side of your pipe about an inch farther down than the window. Now play the notes, and you will find the whole scale has risen a fraction. Bore a second hole to the right of the first, and the scale is raised again. A third hole may be added between the first two, but a little lower down. By this time the pipe is speaking nearly a semi-tone higher than at first. To close the holes make tiny pegs of match-stick and push them in, allowing them to project, so that they may be withdrawn at need.

Another useful addition to your pipe will be a window blind. This is made by sewing a strip of narrow washing elastic into a band, and by drawing it over the mouth-piece until it rests just above the window. When the scale sounds sharp, pull the blind down over part of the window; this closes it a little and the scale is a fraction lowered. The pegs and window blind are shown in Diagram 7.

PLAYING A PIPE WHEN IT IS MADE

The holes must be firmly covered to make the key-note, admitting no modicum of air. Place the first three fingers of each hand on the six finger holes, the left hand being uppermost. Each hole must be felt separately, and firmly pressed, *using the centre of the top finger joint, and keeping the tip well flattened on the pipe.* Beginners are apt to use the tips to cover the holes rather than the flattened fingers, and in this way air is admitted and the note wavers or squeaks. The thumb hole is pressed firmly with the thumb of the left hand.

Blow very gently with all the holes covered. This gives the key-note, or D.

E. Open the first hole.

F♯. Open the second hole as well as the first.

G. Open first, second and third holes.

A. Open first four holes.

B. Open first five holes.

C♯. Open all six holes.

D. Open all six finger holes and also the thumb hole.

E. This is obtained, as a rule, by opening the first hole, as if for the lower E, but by blowing rather harder. If it seems flat, open also the thumb hole, or thumb hole together with the top finger hole. If sharp, close first, second, fourth and fifth holes only.

F♯. May be obtained by cross-fingering, and sometimes further notes of the scale as well, but this varies for each pipe and must be discovered by the player. Half notes will come at any step of the scale by placing half the finger-tip across the hole instead of closing it, or by forked fingering. This may be studied from a chart.

I think it is advisable at this point to deal with the difficulties the pipe-maker is likely to meet. You will find it better not to read this summary until some difficulty actually assails you which has not already been mentioned. Then you may find it helpful to seek for a cure. I have divided the list into two parts : (A) Difficulties in obtaining a Good Note, and (B) Difficulties in Tuning and in Making the Scale.

A.—DIFFICULTIES IN OBTAINING A GOOD NOTE.
1.—*A Note that Will Not Come.*

The causes are :—

(a) No window-slit, owing to the height and pressure of the cork. File the floor.

(b) A tiny window. Open it with a knife.

(c) Too large an opening, giving a deep window-slit and *arch of the sill.* This is owing to an ill-fitting cork, or one from which too much has been cut. Try replacing the cork by another from which much less is removed to make the passage. If the cork tapers too much, the tapering end may be cut off.

(d) Too deep a passage roof in the bamboo, i.e. too high a ceiling. Shave away the inner surface of the bamboo on each side of the passage roof. Use a larger cork if necessary.

(e) Sawdust or a splinter in the passage. Remove it.

(f) A rounded passage roof. Square the walls and file the ceiling. Be sure that the passage is neatly finished and squared at the point where it reaches the window.

(g) A passage roof *narrower* than the window. Widen the ceiling until it is exactly right. The passage, in *width*, *must* be a continuation of the window. This is most important.

2.—*A Vanishing Note.*

The causes are :—

(a) The swelling of the cork due to moisture. Remove cork and slightly lower floor.

(b) A " stranger " in the passage. Remove cork and wipe it. Make ceiling smooth.

(c) A crack. This may be serious, and happens in frosty weather or in centrally-heated rooms. Cover it completely with adhesive tape, or fill it with glue. Decoration will finally cement and hide deficiencies. Do not leave your pipe on the piano, or near a stove.

3.—*A Note that Sounds an Octave too High, and is Reluctant to Descend on its Own Key.*

The causes are :—

(a) Too small an opening as in 1 (a) above. File the floor at window slit.

(b) Too small a window, as in 1 (b) above. Open it.

(c) Too thin a bamboo, i.e. too small a bore. The effect of too thin a bamboo for a treble pipe may be modified by filing the passage floor, and opening the " window."

4.—*A Thin Note.*

The causes are :—

(a) Too small an opening, as in 1 (a) and 3 (a). File the floor.

(b) Too small a window, as in 1 (b) and 3 (b). Open it.

(c) Thin bamboo, as in 3 (c). Undercut the sill, file the floor and open the window.

(d) A very shallow passage roof. Deepen it, making the ceiling rather higher. A passage roof should be quite one-twentieth of an inch deep.

5.—*A Hoarse or Husky Note.*

The causes are :—

(a) Too large an opening, as in 1 (c). Choose another cork or file the sides of the one already in use. It is often a cure to cut off the cork's tapering end and use its thicker base.

(b) Too deep a bamboo passage, as in 1 (d). A common fault. File the surface of bamboo on each side of passage.

(c) Too large a window, especially in depth. Push the cork farther in. Keep the window slit very fine; the arch of the sill in this case should be almost invisible.

(d) A " stranger " in the passage, as in 1 (e) and 2 (b). Remove it.

(e) A rounded passage roof in the bamboo, as in 1 (f). Make it square.

(f) A passage narrower than the window, as in 1 (g). Widen it to the right size.

(g) A rough passage. File it.

(h) Flaws or breaks in the cork, either in the passage or at the window-slit. If these cannot be cut or filed away, use another cork.

(i) One of the common mistakes in passage floors, as shown in Diagram 5.

Mistakes to avoid at all costs because their cure is difficult.

(a) Too large, and especially too *deep* a window.

(b) Too deep a passage roof, i.e. too high a ceiling.

(c) Use of bamboo with too thick walls.

(d) A thin bamboo, i.e. with too small a bore.

(e) A crack : use adhesive tape.

Final Caution.—In case of an unsatisfactory note examine the window slit, which must be fine but distinctly visible between the cork and bamboo at the head of the window. Also examine the arch of the sill.

B.—DIFFICULTIES IN TUNING AND IN MAKING THE SCALE.

1. *The Key-Note.*

A pipe cut too short, which sounds a sharp note. Build in the sides of the base with plastic wood or cork. This closes the aperture of the pipe and so lowers its pitch.

N.B.—This cannot be done after the holes are made; it is a cure for the pipe at Stage VI.

2.—*The Holes.*

(a) Extra large holes.

If the first hole becomes large before it can be sounded in tune, place the second farther up the pipe than was originally intended, fitting the third into a small space.

(b) The appearance of a squeaking harmonic note when we try to blow the last two steps of the scale.

This occurs more often in treble than in bass pipes and is due to a wrong proportion in the size of the holes. Be careful to avoid placing the first three holes too high. The key of the pipe will have to be altered by slicing half an inch from its base. The first two holes can then be enlarged to bring the scale to tune. This is the only cure, and it sacrifices key.

Sometimes a squeaking harmonic is due to placing the last three holes too near the window.

(c) Husky top notes.

Due to the fit of the cork. The passage floor at the arch of the sill may be found to droop at the sides. The cork must fit tightly at the window, and be straight across the passage floor from side to side. Husky top notes sometimes occur when we place the sixth finger hole or thumb hole too high on the pipe.

3.—*Variations of Pitch after the Pipe is Made.*

(a) Flat Scale.

Draw out a peg. Make a new peg hole. Draw the cork out very slightly. Enlarge the window a little, if its measurement allows. In severe cases, cut a small portion from the base; then the first three holes will have to be enlarged to correspond. If they are already large, this plan is unwise.

(b) Sharp Scale.

Draw down the window blind. Push the cork a little farther in. Substitute another cork which leaves less room in the passage, and which narrows the window slit. Cool the pipe in the open air or run cold water through it. (This is only a temporary measure).

(c) Single notes flat after use.

This is due to swelling in the wood or the presence of wood splinters inside the holes. Enlarge the holes with a knife or rimer bit.

(d) Single notes made too sharp.

Fill holes that are too large with plastic wood, building it in round the walls until the notes are sufficiently flattened.

(e) Pipes in the band out of tune.

Ask every piper to play his scale, if possible comparing it with a piano. Draw a peg or bore a hole in the flat pipes, lower the window blind in the sharp ones. This does not take long and is a necessary precaution before any combined demonstration of pipe-playing. Remember, however, that all pipes will become sharper when they have become " blown in " and that the same will occur in a crowded room.

CHAPTER IV.

ALTO AND TENOR PIPES.

THE ALTO PIPE.

This is a pipe made in the key of A. In length and pitch it lies midway between the treble and tenor pipes, and its chief function is to play the middle voice in three-part music. It is also a sweet solo pipe.

Cut a length of 16 inches with a bore $\frac{7}{8}$—1 inch inside diameter and tune it to A after the mouth piece is made. Otherwise the directions for a treble pipe may be followed, except that the window is made a little larger, i.e. $\frac{1}{4} \times \frac{5}{16}$ inches. A gap of about $1\frac{1}{2}$ inches is advisable between the first three and the last three holes. This gap may vary, for the last finger hole is measured roughly $3\frac{3}{4}$ inches. from the window.

THE TENOR PIPE.

Cut a length of 24 inches, with an inside diameter of about $1\frac{1}{4}$ inches. Stage I and Stage II are the same as they were in the first chapter, except that the window of Stage II is larger, the measurement being $\frac{5}{16}$ of an inch down, by $\frac{3}{8}$ across. The sill is longer than in treble or alto; it is carried down the face of the pipe one inch, measured from the top, or edge. This gives a long slant that must be smoothly made, the surface shaved away gradually and filed to an even surface. The top or edge of the sill should be cut as sharp as possible without weakening the wood and the sides cut exactly to the same width as the window. The window slit must be fine. The first note, when the cork has been sufficiently filed, is mellow and deep, while several harmonics are forthcoming when you blow a little harder.

In tuning the key-note to D (one octave below the treble pipe), you will find it necessary to cut away longer pieces. Remove $1\frac{1}{2}$ inches for a tone, $\frac{3}{4}$ of an inch for a semi-tone. This is safe, and you may find that even more is necessary.

The first hole should be meaured a fraction higher up than before. Mark the quarter as usual, but place the hole $\frac{1}{8}$ of an inch above this. It is also well to remember that you should place the holes higher upon an extra wide pipe than upon a narrow one.

The placing of a tenor's scale needs caution. If, while you are working, you perceive that the lowest hole is becoming large in order to achieve the second step of the scale, place the first three notes far apart.

If the reverse happens, the note will leap to its place while the first hole is quite small; in this case make the three steps nearer together. Apart from these warnings, the average measurement between the holes is one inch, from centre to centre.

The holes fall into two groups of three. Mark all these out before you make them. Between the first three and the last three a large gap should be left, and the last finger hole is marked $6\frac{3}{4}$ inches from the centre of the window. The other two in the second group are measured from it. The thumb hole may be placed $\frac{3}{4}$ of an inch higher than the last finger hole.

Pegs and a window blind should be added, but the pegs will not have so great an effect of altering pitch as in the case of a smaller pipe. The Tenor's tuning-range is little more than quarter of a tone.

The bamboo tenor is a beautiful and subtle pipe, but it must be practised before it shows its full capacity of tone. It improves with age and with use.

FLUTES, RECORDERS, VIOLS, DRUMS and EXTENDED PIPES.

It will be seen in the illustration that the children are making and playing instruments other than the pipes described here. It has always been the aim of the Pipers' Guild to encourage the making of musical instruments. Flutes, recorders, viols and drums have been included and it is now possible to make treble, alto and tenor pipes which give a much larger range of notes. This handbook is only a first step. If you wish to know more you should join the community of the Pipers' Guild, the Society which originated from those simple experiments and in which the full musical implications are realised.

CHAPTER V.

MUSICAL TRAINING IN THE PIPERS' BAND

WITH our pipes we find endless opportunity for musical training. It is not wise to be dogmatic about method, for every teacher should be free to develop his own ideas and to add his experience to the common store. Yet there is a foundation already proved by experience and others may build upon it. This chapter is added to help teachers to see their own way clearly. It is derived from experience with pupils, whether children or grown-up people, who have come to the lessons with pocket knives and enthusiasm, but with no musical knowledge.

There is a guiding principle which must underlie every effort we make. " Pipes " do not constitute a music lesson apart from other lessons ; they are not to be treated as an isolated " *subject* " in education. Their chief value lies in the fact that they correlate three arts, hand-work design and music, and that by doing so, they bring out the hidden capacities which are the heritage of every man alive. In fact, the activity of each art is used to express and to explain the other two. Again, the pipe band must be related as closely as possible to education as a whole, or it will be comparatively worthless. Its rhythmic music should be allied to rhythmic bodily movement, its hand-work to the science of sound or acoustics, its melodies to history and drama, its improvisations to the metre of poetry. These are examples to illustrate the true principle of unity in education which is probably the only solution to the " lack of time " problem in schools. We want to give more and more to our children and this growing sense of responsibility on their behalf involves many isolated subjects, each one in its half hour and department, unrelated to the rest. The children's minds are shifted rapidly from subject to subject so that there can be no continuity of thought. The musical child waits impatiently for the music lesson, the craftsman sighs for the handwork hour. No one is allowed to feel that the best things are as much at unity as life itself, and that they should be enjoyed by all.

Before leaving generalities to speak of the pipes, let us turn aside to consider an ideal combination which could occupy a single day and break down this system of departments.

Puppetry is another craft which is inclusive and unifying. The child who makes and dresses a puppet and manipulates it in a play to express history or literature, or both, is combining many so-called " subjects." He is learning craftsmanship, painting, drawing, history expressed in costume as well as in the subject of the play and literature in the words he uses as the puppet's spokeman. Here, history and literature are both expressed in dramatic action. An ideal orchestra for the puppet drama is provided in the shape of a hand-made pipe band and to all those aspects of education already considered, we have added a new craft, allied in its turn to design and music-making. The whole is continuous, creative, vividly interesting and united. After this suggestion it will not be too great a shock if I say that music making in the pipe band should begin in the hand-work room.

Musical training starts early and the pipe-maker learns to judge the tone of his pipe when he blows its first note. Care and good craftsmanship will result in the delicious *feeling* of good tone which is also to be heard and appreciated when it is blown. Exquisitely pure tone is the reward of a good craftsman and the goal of every pipe-maker. In these days of second-hand music and second-rate sound, critical appreciation of tone is something to achieve ; a real part of musical training.

When the key-note of a pipe is pitched, intensive ear training begins and this is continuous during the process of carving a scale. Very little extra comment is necessary to explain why. Every pipe-maker recognises his own achievement in this respect and the results have been proved over and over again. Astonishing development comes. The apparently unmusical pupil grasps the meaning of a scale in the most natural way and in time he finds the power to make melody. The training of ear and hand together as the scale is made, overlaps the first steps in reading from staff notation, together with the mastery of fingering. When two holes are finished in the pipe, we learn to play the first three notes of the scale and to call them by their numbers—1, 2 and 3, placed on a staff of five lines. A little tune should be played perfectly on these three notes before another hole is made. The process is repeated when the next hole is finished and again when four holes are pitched and half the scale becomes available. This is a case of " more haste, less speed " and the teacher should not hurry on. Each stage in the making should be made perfectly clear and it is a great mistake to postpone learning to play until the pipe is finished. The process will then be much more confusing and much less sure. After the mastery of four holes, however, the other three may be finished in one sitting for they are easier both to pitch and to play.

This system, especially the use of numbers, which lead the piper to staff notation by very quick and simple stages, is described in Book I of " Pipers' Music in three Stages," published by Cramer.

Meanwhile, the piper may write the numbers in another order, placing them on five lines in a little manuscript book, enclosing them in bar lines like his pattern and playing them to himself. This is the earliest step of all to composition and it may take place while his companions are " catching up." When all are ready, the orchestra combines in simple phrases to include the number of holes that are finished, the piano adding a soft accompaniment.

Rhythmic movement, stepping, tapping, etc. may emphasis the character of these phrases, and a minim pause may be made at the " half-way house " on a 2 or a 5. When the first set of pipes in **D** Major is finished, the craftsman is ready for his music lessons in the school orchestra. He learns to read complete melodies and descants in **D** Major, still using the system of numbers to consolidate his sense of pitch. When he knows five or six little tunes, various in mood and pace, he makes a new pipe in the hand-work room. It is pitched to the A below his **D** pipe (the middle or alto pipe of Chapter III), and he will be able to make the whole scale without pause, for he has already mastered simple technique and the playing of his new instrument will present no difficulty.

In the orchestra he will now learn a new melody, pitched to A. The numbers are dropped on the Staff to correspond to the longer pipe with its lower pitch and the player will get his first idea of what is meant by change of key. He will also revel in the mellow depth and beauty of his new pipe. This is the last tune to be played from numbers : real notation is used henceforward and will be easily understood. The way is cleared for melodies in other keys on the same pipe, major or minor. The alto pipe is followed by the tenor, pitched an octave below the treble. Then the orchestra has opportunity to play in three or more parts unaccompanied and the bass clef is introduced.

Meanwhile, the piper should find himself a ready improvisor on all the instruments he makes. Indeed, his pipes prove an unexpectedly easy means to improvisation. He is himself astonished to find that little tunes of his own making come perfectly naturally. A hidden capacity is brought to light, for composition ceases to be the mystery it is to the child who can only use singing to give expression to an idea. The pipe itself seems to assume responsibility and to make a tune almost before the player is aware of it.

In leading children to appreciate the elements of form through their own improvisations I suggest three ways which may all be used in the same pipers' band. They are not offered as completed schemes but as a foundation of experience on which we may build our own methods.

The first constitutes part of learning to play while the pipes are being made, the second is improvisation on repeated rhythmic patterns and the third uses the rhythm of poetry to suggest a tune. Improvisation and rhythmic work move forward together, side by side.

The first way of improvising has been suggested already. It consists in making little four bar tunes on the model of one already learned, to cover the number of finished holes. In each tune there is a minim pause at the end of the second bar to mark the half-way house. When only two or three holes are made we must use the super tonic for this pause, but when the fourth appears we may rest halfway upon the dominant. We can write our tunes as they are made and the band can divide into sections to express them alternately in music or in rhythmic movement. Here Dr. Yorke Trotter's rhythmic method has helped us to see more clearly and we have still much to learn from him.

When the pipes are finished, time values may be learned by playing the Exercises for Pipes published by Curwens. We pass from simple pulse measures, written in crotchets, to repeated patterns, in which minim, quaver and semi-quaver appear. The minim, for instance, is introduced as the final beat of every bar in an ascending sequence, ♩ ♩ 𝅗𝅥 , ♩ ♩ 𝅗𝅥 , ♩ ♩ 𝅗𝅥 A new conductor is chosen from the orchestra at each lesson: he is given a chance to beat time and maintain the measure of four in each bar. The exercise is usually played in two parts, treble and alto, but treble D pipes are used for both parts. When it is mastered the teacher, or one of the children, plays ♩ ♩ 𝅗𝅥 alone, but this time on a new change of notes, improvised. He then commands the orchestra to answer all together in the same pattern, while he conducts. No one is self-conscious about this, for there is no chance of being heard individually in the general piping that follows. It is a harmless confusion of soft tones, not unlike a chorus of birds and the confidence it gives justifies the method. Each piper has improvised his own bar. When this experience has been repeated two or three times individual members of the band will be able to pipe questions alone, calling upon other individuals to answer them.

This method is developed as we pass on to more difficult patterns. Here is a little sentence which is repeated in the exercise on different notes, ♩ ♫♩ ♩, ♩ ♩ 𝅗𝅥 It can be treated in exactly the same way. First it may be impressed on the piper's mind by stepping, tapping or movement of any kind.

The class may be divided into sections, one to conduct the beat and the other to tap the pattern and these groups exchange activities at a word while the piano is playing the exercise. Then the tune is learned on the pipes, reading from the staff with a conductor. Finally it is improvised upon. Thus, time training and improvisation are blended.

There is still a third method. Poetry written in simple metre may be read aloud. Each line will suggest a simple musical sentence, and a piper will be found in the class to improvise it, while another will write the notes on a board from his dictation. If the verse be one of four lines, we shall come to a suitable half-way house at the end of the second, and we judge the whole when the entire verse has been changed into music, asking the pipers to criticise their own work and to suggest improvements. The tune is then played by the band as a complete melody, the work of four improvisors. Remarkably soon, each individual piper will be able to improvise the whole of a verse without pause for thought. His experience of tunes which he has learned to appreciate in the band will give him various rhythms in which to do this. The indication of $\frac{6}{8}$ time by singing to a swing of the arms will be enough to set a child going; theorising on the number of beats in the bar will be simply waste of time. A little girl piper in this remote, unmusical village where I write, said, when she had improvised a number of $\frac{6}{8}$ lines in a single breath, "When you once begin, you can't stop." It is, indeed, perfectly natural. The tunes may be written, line by line, as they are composed. Sometimes the blackboard is useful and at others the children's own manuscript books are used. When a particularly happy melody occurs, the whole band of pipers may transcribe it into music books and, with a simple pianoforte accompaniment improvised by the teacher, it becomes part of the permanent repertoire.

At this point, when we link poetry with pipe music, something should be said about the blend of pipes and voices. In part playing it will often be found helpful to divide the orchestra into singers and players. Treble and alto voices may take part in combined music-making. So far very few experiments of this kind have been made, but the sound of singing with pipe music in harmony, promises to be very beautiful.

Time training has been explored in the rhythmic exercises and the improvisations based on them. Rhythm in a wider sense comes when we link pipe music with rhythmic movement. Eurythmics and every kind of beautiful dancing should contribute to the result. Country dance tunes are at their very best when they are piped and the lovely rhythm of English folk music when it is played for the dancers becomes part of the piper himself. He may put aside his pipe when he is tired of one occupation and change places with the dancer. In this way he shares alternately in music and in dance.

The art of playing well leads to expression in the pipe band. This is of a subtle and delicate nature and is not to be obtained by loud crescendo or perceptible diminuendo, which only results in sharp or in flat playing. Expression of a less obvious and more educational kind comes through the phrasing of music. This is done with the tongue.

Normally, each note is started by a touch of the tongue. It is brought against the back of the teeth with the gentle sound of " te," pronounced without effort. Two notes would give the effect of " te, te " not of " ha, ha " or of " pe, pe." The lips are not used at all. The first note of any phrase should take a stronger tonguing than the others. Two or more notes may be blown under one tonguing which gives the effect of a combined legato group, but the groups are usually in pairs and very seldom more than three in number. Thus, a couple of quavers may be tongued " te, te," when we want a staccato effect, or " te-re " when a legato is better. Between the two, many devices are possible. We may use our tongues so softly that the separate notes are only just perceptibly apart or we may pronounce them "te-the" These are nearly legato but not entirely so.

The regulation of tone is managed almost entirely by the tongue, which controls the amount of breath sent into our pipes and shuts off the surplus blowing which is the cause of a husky note, or of swooping. It also regulates expression. The mood of the music appears in the character of the tonguing and shades of subtle expression can be controlled. Inevitably, the expert piper reveals his character, his imagination and his taste. The phrasing given by any composer to his own music may be interpreted by the pipers' band. If no phrasing appears, the band chooses its own. A simple piece of music may be altered completely in mood by changes and new combinations of phrasing.

A little table of musical training will recapitulate and will make this chapter clear to the teacher.

The Appreciation of Tone.

By the feeling and sound of a perfect note produced by good craftsmanship.

Intensive Pitch Training.

By carving each note in the pipe to the right size, and by listening for the right moment to stop.

Sight Reading.

By learning from numbers on a Staff and then by reading from notation. By making six pipes to cover all the keys.

Time Training.

By learning the note values in rhythmic exercises and their combination in simple time measures. By conducting.

Rhythm.

By linking pipe music with all forms of rhythmic movement and dancing.

Expression and Appreciation.

By shades of expressive phrasing in the interpretation of really good music.

Improvisation and Appreciation.

(a) By writing, playing and stepping little tunes a each stage of making a scale in the pipe.

(b) By improvising musical sentences in question and answer, based on patterns in the rhythmic exercises.

(c) By using the rhythm of poetry to suggest melody.

Individual adventures and experiments in education should follow. No two people will develop pipe-making and playing in the same way.

CHAPTER VI.

THE DECORATION OF MUSICAL PIPES
by NORA GIBBS.

From people listening to and looking at pipes, I have heard one comment that was complete: it was "The pipers have made their instruments which have such a sweet tone and which, when you look at them, are works of art." This chapter, then, deals with the "works of art."

The pipe, made and tuned, is complete as regards its musical purpose, but it needs individuality. It must be your own instrument, not just "a bamboo pipe."

The following ways and means may help you to this end, but there must be many other ways in decoration that have not yet been tried.

Style in decoration should come from the tool you are using. A pen will give an entirely different design from a brush, and a scratch from something applied. Successful ways of pipe decoration I have seen, are painting, pen and ink, carving, scratching and filing, appliqué (with bamboo, pewter or paper) and poker work.

HOLES   NORMAN PILLAR   FROG SPAWN

In whatever way you are decorating, there are a few general principles which will help you to good design. First, remember you are designing a pipe, not something flat. Therefore, lines *round* it will always be right, for they emphasise the roundness. The Primitive is content to go round his pipe with bands of different designs from end to end, leaving some carefully considered empty spaces. The western development of " the rings round " is a spiral, which goes round and *down*—a harder thing to do, but very beautiful. Think of a maypole ; its interlaced spirals : and of all the variations possible.

You may, however, wish to start with the holes. If so, decorate round each hole first with some little pattern, then try to connect each piece together, and so make a whole design. The connection may be one line, straight or wandering, or it may be two or three lines. The same design round each hole will give a fine, severe effect, restful and coherent (if a little repetitive) but you may prefer to alternate two designs (which, in result, will be lighter), or even put a different design round each hole. This last plan will need some severe connecting line, to give it stability.

" But what is our design to be ?" you may ask. If in doubt, keep to simple, geometric shapes, i.e. the triangle, diamond, square or circle. When you want connecting lines, use " spotting " or " criss-crossing," so that the spaces are neither too solid nor too empty. Many of the best designs have been made of these simple, fundamental shapes. Meanwhile, one shape, repeated at regular intervals all over a pipe, will give you what is called an " all-over pattern."

Anything may suggest design to you—a flower, a leaf, cobwebs, frogspawn and even people : but try to think out a simple way of showing the shape, then repeat it somehow, give it colour : —and it is complete.

Bamboo is a very beautiful background and it is not necessary to cover it up with an all-over colour, unless you really wish to. If it is in spaces not too large, it gives pleasant texture and colour in design, and it may even be counter-changed with solid colour. This is a good and " stylish " use of bamboo. In designing, do not forget the back of the pipe ; it is best to spread out the pattern so that it goes round, even if only at the bottom and at the thumb-hole.

As regards colour, do not take advice. Choose what you want and what you like. There are beautiful pipes in bright colours and there are equally good ones in black. Colour is a very personal thing.

Whatever method of decoration you use, rub the pipe well with sandpaper first and all over. Painting may be with enamels but the best results I have seen were done with powder colour or poster colour.

 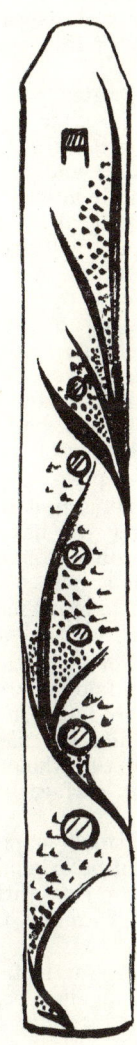 

BANDS   SPIRAL   ALL-OVER

The paint must be applied just opaque and no more and must not be laid on thick like enamel but spread like water colour. Poster colours can be bought in small tubes at threepence or pots at sixpence, or in larger quantities. Powder colours can be bought in tins at a shilling and these go a very long way. They should be of the kind that only needs water for mixing and should be mixed to the consistency of thin cream and used with a not too-full brush.

Not all water colour is water proof, of course: you must varnish the pipe or shellac it, after it has been decorated with powder or paste colour. Spirit varnish can be bought in small bottles (sevenpence ha'-penny) and one coat is enough. Your brush must be washed in methylated spirit. You must be very sure that the painting has really dried out, before the varnish or shellac is applied, or your pipe will peel! Shellac is obtainable at a chemist. Crush two ounces of orange shellac into a pint of methylated spirit and leave it to dissolve (twenty-four hours); shake a little and apply one coat at a time, leaving each coat to dry hard before applying the next. Each coat will give a harder gloss to the pipe and at least six should be given. This sounds more arduous than it is and the result is well worth the trouble When "hard up" I have bought half an ounce of shellac and a quarter of meths from a chemist of the humbler sort—total cost threepence, for about a dozen pipes.

For pen and ink design, it is best to give the pipe a coat of size (from the oil shop), after you have sandpapered it. Leave this to dry and then use ordinary, twopenny coloured inks for your design and draw with a pen. You will need varnish or shellac to waterproof the whole pipe finally. Some people shellac the inside of their pipes too: with advantage, I believe.

Carving, the next method of decorating, has many possibilities. You may carve with a penknife or scratch with it or you may file designs. Colour may be introduced into the uncarved parts or put, with a pen or brush, into the filed marks. Another very satisfactory plan is to colour the whole pipe and then cut or file away designs on the coloured surface. This reveals the bamboo again.

For appliqué decoration, small shapes in bamboo may be cut out and stuck on (with seccotine or similar substance), wherever you think they will be decorative without being in the way: then, design may be built up around them. The effect, if you like, can be quite barbaric.

On metal pipes (the bass, for instance) only enamel paints are possible, but scratching is again a possibility (as in engraving) and ribbons may be tied round, to give effect and colour.

Decorated pipes need care, when they are carried about; if they are allowed to jostle each other, they may chip. Make coloured cases of material or of knitted wools, to keep them safe. The cases may be decorated, too.

NORA GIBBS.

THE PIPERS' GUILD.

To further the Craft, threefold, of Making, Decorating, Playing, each man his own instrument.

President :—R. VAUGHAN WILLIAMS, Mus. Doc., O.M.

Director :—Miss MARGARET JAMES, 7, Blenheim Drive, Oxford.

Secretary :—Mrs. RIGG, Meadowrise, Stocksmead, Washington, Sussex.

WHY SHOULD I MAKE MY OWN PIPE?

Making Pipes is a musical adventure. You will delight in the discovery of sound and in building your own scale. Your pipe will equal any that you can buy, both in range and in tone. It will be less expensive.

WHERE CAN I LEARN TO MAKE A PIPE?

At one of the organised groups of the Pipers' Guild. I can also learn by private tuition or by correspondence. Write to the Secretary for details.

DO I NEED TO BE A CRAFTSMAN OR A MUSICIAN TO BE ABLE TO MAKE A PIPE?

No.

IS THERE ANY MUSIC PUBLISHED FOR PIPES?

Yes. Write to Messrs. J. B. Cramer & Co., Official Publishers to the Guild, 139, New Bond St., W.1., or to Messrs. Novello, Curwen, Paxton, Schott.

WHAT IS THE PURPOSE OF THE GUILD?

To encourage the threefold experience of making, decorating and playing pipes and to ensure in it the highest musical standard.

HOW DID THE GUILD START?

It was founded and is directed by Miss Margaret James.

WHERE DOES THE GUILD EXTEND?

National Branches are established in many countries throughout the world.

WHAT ARE THE QUALIFICATIONS FOR GUILD MEMBERSHIP?

A member must have made his own pipe, must agree to the use of simple tools prescribed by the Guild, and must promise not to buy or sell pipes.

WHAT IS AN ASSOCIATE MEMBER?
These share in most of the Guild amenities, but do not make their own pipes.

HOW CAN I JOIN THE GUILD?
The subscription if 7/6 a year. Write to the Secretary, (see front page.)

WHAT ARE THE PRIVILEGES OF GUILD MEMBERSHIP?
1. The exchange of discoveries in materials, music and experience.
2. Members receive "The Piping Times' Journal of the Pipers Guild with regular news of vacation schools, classes and all activities.
3. Reduced rates for groups.
4. Participation in Rallies.
5. Open doors of hospitality, from Pipers all over the world.

TEACHERS. The Guild trains teachers who, on passing the Journeyman examination, are qualified to teach pipe-making and playing under Guild recommendation. There is also an Advanced examination.

PUPLICATIONS FOR THE PIPES

TEXT BOOKS
Works by MARGARET JAMES

THE PIPERS' GUILD HANDBOOK is the Official Text Book of the Pipers' Guild. It describes the origin of the movement and gives full Directions and Diagrams for Making and Playing Pipes .. 2s. 6d.
FRENCH EDITION—LE MANUAL DES FAISEURS DE PIPEAUX. *Translated by Madame Gueritte* .. .. .. 2s. 6d.
DIRECTIONS FOR MAKING THE BASS PIPE. (*With Diagrams by* NORA GIBBS) .. .. *Net Cash* 6d.
DIRECTIONS FOR MAKING EXTENDED TREBLE AND ALTO PIPES (*With Diagrams*). (*Recorder Scale*). .. *Net Cash* 6d.
TUTOR FOR THE BAMBOO PIPE .. Treble, Alto and Tenor 1s. 6d.

Work by R. C. BARNES

THE PIPERS' DRUMS.. .. .. 2s. 0d.
Instructions for making Drums and Tambourines, and four pages of explicit diagrams.

PIPERS' MUSIC by Margaret James

MUSIC BOOKS IN THREE STAGES—Progressive material to be used in conjunction with "The Pipers' Guild Handbook."
Book 1. Large Size *with Piano Accompaniment* .. .. .. 2s. 0d.
    1a. Small Size, *Pipe part only* .. .. 9d.
Book 2. Large Size *with Piano Acc. (second part optional)* .. 2s. 6d.
    2a. Small Size, *Pipe part only* .. .. 1s. 0d.
Book 3. Three-part Tunes for Pipes (*Treble, Alto and Tenor*) .. 9d.

SOLOS for Treble Pipes with P.F. acc.

Book 1. Pipers Music .. .. .. arr. Margaret James	2s.	0d.
Book Ia. ,, ,, pipe part only ,, ,,		9d.
Twenty-two Airs for Treble Pipe (with descant) —a book for beginners ,, ,,	2s.	6d.
,, ,, ,, pipe part only		9d.
National Airs for Pipers (with solf-fa) arr. by Marion Anderson	2s.	0d.
,, ,, ,, pipe part only		9d.
Nursery Rhymes for Pipers or Singers (with sol-fa) ,, ,,	2s.	0d.
,, ,, ,, ,, pipe part only		9d.
Pipe a Merry Tune (Voice-Pipes-Rhythmic) ,, ,, ,,	1s.	0d.
Rhythmic Work for Pipers (with sol-fa) ,, ,, ,,	2s.	0d.
,, ,, ,, Pipe part only		9d.
Ten German Folk Tunes .. .. ,, ,, ,,	1s.	0d.
A Pipers' March (For Pipes. (*Percussion ad. lib.*) and Piano) .. .. .. by Kathleen M. Blocksidge	2s.	0d.

Score and Piano 1/-. *Score* 6d. *Extra Parts* 2d.

Graded Beginners' Tunes .. by Kathleen M. Blocksidge, each (for particulars see page 42)		3d.
Piper's Posy (A) .. .. by Denis Capes	1s.	0d.
Canons for Treble Pipes.. .. .. .. by Imogen Holst	1s.	0d.
Young Guards' March (for Pipes (*Percussion ad. lib.*) and Piano) by John Martin		

Score and Piano 1s. net, *Pipe* (& extra parts) 4d. each, *Score* 1s. *Complete Set* 3s. net.

Trebles All (Twelve Songs in Two Parts for Voice and Pipes) arr. Annie Z. Miller	2s.	6d.
Trebles All, Pipe and Voice Parts with words		9d.
Pipers of Eireann (Cead Mile Failte) Fifteen Irish Tunes for Solo Pipes with P.F. acc. Trios and Quartets, arr. Annie Z. Miller	2s.	0d.
Chansons Populaires Francaises. 24 Airs for One or Two Treble, 5 Duets, Treble and Alto, 3 Easy Trios, arr. Annie Z. Miller net	3s.	6d.
,, ,, ,, Pipe Parts only	1s.	6d.
French-Canadian Folk Tunes (Unison and Two-Part) arr. Edith Rowland	1s.	6d.
,, ,, ,, ,, Pipe Parts only		9d.
Telegraph Poles (*Voice, Piano, Percussion Band and Pipes*) by Cyril Winn	2s.	0d.

Leaflets (see pages 41, 42)—Nos. 12, 17, 23, 26, 27, 28, 30, 43, 44.

Leaflets for Classwork.

Come live with me (2 pt.Canon for Treble Pipes and/or Voices) by Henry Cooke				4d.
Pan Pipes	,,	,,	,,	4d.
Shepherd on a Hill	,,	,,	,,	4d.
Sing ! Sing ye birds	,,	,,	,,	4d.
Easy Tunes for Treble Pipe only .. .. arr. Hester Girdlestone				

No. 1. Traditional Tunes and Songs of other Lands.
No. 2. Rounds. No. 3. Negro and Plantation Songs.
24 Copies for 2/- (or 2d. per copy each number).

DUETS for Treble and Alto Pipes with P.F. acc.

Book II. Pipers' Music.. .. .. .. arr. Margaret James	2.	6d.
Book IIa. ,, ,, Pipe Parts only	1s.	0d.
Tom, Dick and Harry (for 2 Treble, 1 Alto) .. by Denis Capes	1s.	0d.
Two Duets—(a) Bouree, (b) The Tarn (leaflet No. 16) by Eva Pain ..		6d.
*Two Duets by Bach (a) Bouree, (b) Minuett (leaflet No. 29) arr, Olga Peppercorn		4d.
Lullaby (Brahms) 2 Treble Pipes .. .. arr. A. M. Scott		4d.
Chansons Populaires Francaises (see above)		

*For an Adjusted Pipe

SOLOS and DUETS for the Alto Pipe and Piano

Morning Song (leaflet No. 21).. .. .. by Richard Hall	4d.
Alto Airs (Solos and Duets) ..orig. and arr. by Annie Z. Miller	2s. 0d.
,, ,, ,, ,, Pipe Parts only ,, ,,	9d.
Pipers of Eireann (see page 39) .. .. ,, ,,	2s. 0d.
Pipers of Scotland	
Duets for 1st and 2nd Alto Pipes (or as Solos) ,, ,,	1s. 0d.

VARIOUS Combinations of Pipes

*Two Classical Airs (leaflet No. 13) .. .. arr. Elsa Boyd	4d.
(a) Allegro (Mozart) for Treble and Tenor	
(b) Passepied (Bach) Treble, Alto, Tenor	
Early in the Morning (leaflet No. 25) 2 Tenor and Bass	
by Denis Capes	4d.
Tom, Dick and Harry (3 Short Trios) 2 Treble and 1 Alto ,, ,,	1s. 0d.
The Cuckoo Clock—Duet for 2 Treble (or 2 Alto, using treble	
fingering) or 2 Tenor .. .. .. by Richard Hall	4d.
*My Bairn, Sleep Softly Now (Carol for unaccompanied Female	
Voices, S.S.S.A.A. or for Soprano Voices and Pipes)	
by Imogen Holst	9d.
Canon for Treble Pipes (for from 2 to 10 pipes) ,, ,,	1s. 0d.
Two Trios (leaflet No. 22) by Eva Pain	6d.
(a) Scottish Air for Alto, Tenor and Bass	
(b) Flibberty Gibbety, Sarah for Treble, Tenor and Bass	
The Ash Grove (leaflet No. 10)	
for 1st and 2nd Treble, Alto and Tenor .. arr. T. H. Tudbal	4d

TRIOS FOR PIPES
Treble, Alto and Tenor

Book III Pipers' Music.. .. .. arr. Margaret James	9d.
Twelve Simple Trios .. .. .. arr. Dorothy Barnard	2s. 0d.
Twelve More Simple Trios .. .. .. ,, ,,	2s. 0d.
Glees, Catches and Rounds (Trios and Quartets)	
arr. Biedermann-Weber	2s. 0d.
Puppet Suite .. .. by Denis Capes	1s. 0d.
Four Tunes by Bach and Mozart .. arr. Vincent Bradley	1s. 0d.
The Fieldside Suite (with Piano acc. ad. lib. ... by Chris Edmunds	2s. 0d.
,, ,, extra parts (each) .. ,, ,,	4d.
Five Pipe Pieces .. .. .. by Howard Ferguson	2s. 0d.
Five Short Airs on a Ground for Pipes .. by Imogen Holst	2s. 0d.
First Book of Tunes for the Pipes .. .. ,, ,,	2s. 0d.
(Folk Dances and Madrigals set in 2, 3, 4 and 5 parts)	
Second Book of Tunes for the Pipes (in 2, 3 and 4 parts) ,,	2s. 0d.
Twelve Old English Dance Airs	
(from Playford's " English Dancing Master ") arr. ,, ,,	2s. 0d.
Elizabethan Ayres .. .. .. arr. Edgar H. Hunt	2s. 0d.
Ten Short Trios (easy) .. .. .. arr. L. Margerison	1s. 0d.
Pipers of Eireann (see page 39).. .. arr. Annie Z. Miller	2s. 0d.
The Rivenhall Suite for Three Pipes .. by Martin Shaw	1s. 6d.
(In Three Movements in which each Pipe has a melody in turn)	
Dance Movements Book I of 17th and 18th Century Composers	
arr. Millicent Shepperd	2s. 0d.
,, ,, Book II ,, (Trios and Quartets) ,,	2s. 0d.
,, ,, Book III (Trios and Quartets) ,, ,,	2s. 0d.
Six Christmas Carols .. .. ,, ,,	1s. 0d.
Ten Christmas Carols .. .. ,, ,,	1s. 0d.
Petit Suite .. .. by Antonia M. Taufstein	1s. 6d.
Twelve Belgian Folk Songs .. ..arr. ,, ,,	2s. 0d.

Leaflets (see pages 41 and 42) Nos. 1 to 9, 11, 13, 20, 24, 36, 37, 38, 40, 41, 42.
*For an Adjusted Pipe

QUARTETS FOR PIPES
Treble, Alto, Tenor and Bass

*A Folk-tune Suite	.. by Lindsay Bleach	2s. 0d.
Pipe part only	.. ,, ,,	9d.
Quartets Book I..	arr. L. Margerison	1s. 6d.
,, ,, II	,, ,,	1s. 6d.
,, ,, III	,, ,,	1s. 6d.
*Six Pieces by Giles Farnaby ..	arr. Annie Z. Miller	1s. 6d.
Pipers of Eireann (see page 39)	,, ,,	2s. 0d.
*Quartets by Purcell	arr. Margery Olsson	1s. 6d.
*Essex Airs	by Eva Pain	2s. 6d.
*Book II Dance Movements (*Trios and Quartets*)		
	arr. Millicent Shepperd	2s. 0d.
Book III ,, ,, ,, ,,	,, ,,	2s. 0d.
Suite in G (from the works of F. G. Handel)	,, ,,	2s. 6d.
Huit Danses Neerlandaises (16*th Century Danses*)		
	arr. Antonia M. Taufstein	2s. 0d.

CRAMER'S 9d. SERIES OF MUSIC FOR PIPES
Small books with Pipe Parts only for Classes.

Twenty-Two Airs for Treble Pipe ..	..arr. Margaret James	
Trebles All (Pipe and Voice Parts)	,, Annie Z. Miller	
Alto Pipe Airs	,, ,,	
Pipers' Music Book I	,, Margaret James	
,, ,, Book III (*Trios*)	,, ,, ,,	
Rhythmic Work for Pipers (with Solfa)	,, Marion Anderson	
National Airs (with Solfa)	,, ,, ,,	
Nursery Rhymes for Pipers and Singers ..	..,, ,, ,,	
French Canadian Folk Tunes	,, Edith Rowland	
A Folk-tune Suite (Pipes part only) ..	.. by Lindsay Bleach	
Pipers' Tunes (*Duets*) Book II	Margaret James	1s. 0d.
Chanson Populaires Francaises	arr. Annie Z. Miller (net)	1s. 6d.

Editions of the above are published with Pianoforte acc.
excepting Pipers' Music Book III

FAIRY PLAYS FOR CHILD PIPERS (In One Act)

The Pipes of Puck	by Evelyn Peat	1s. 6d.
The Forsaken Fairy	,, ,,	1s. 6d.
Peter Piper .. .. by Anne Harding Thompson		2s. 6d.

Approximate Time of Performance—20 Minutes

CHARTS FOR SCHOOL USE (21 ins. × 31 ins.)

Volkslied and This Old Man ..	arr. Margaret James	9d.
Shepherd's Lullaby	..,, ,, ,,	9d.

LEAFLETS (Net Cash)
Trios are for Treble, Alto and Tenor, unless otherwise stated.

No. 1.	O Gin I were Where Gowdie Runs (Trio)	arr. Blanche Hindson	2d.
No. 2.	Dressmaker, A Carol for Voice and Pipes (original)	Annie Z. Miller	2d.
No. 3.	By Dimpled Brook (Arne) (Trio) ..	arr. Ethel Sidgwick	2d.
No. 4.	Oats and Beans (Lincolnshire Tune) (Trio)	arr. Gertrude Enoch	2d.
No. 5.	Gavotte (Handel) (Trio)	arr. Dorothy Barnard	2d.
No. 6.	Shepherds' Hey (Trio)	arr. Gertrude Enoch	2d.
No. 7.	The Almande (Trio) ..	Heurtley Braithwaite	4d.
No. 8.	The Violet (Scarlatti Trio)	arr. Milicent Shepperd	4d.
No. 9.	An Air for Holsworthy Church Bells (Wesley) (Trio)	arr. Dorothy Barnard	4d.
No. 10.	The Ash Grove (1st and 2nd Treble, Alto and Tenor Pipes)	arr. T. H. Tudbal	4d.

No. 11.	Three Pieces from the "Water Music" (Handel) (Trio)	arr. Eric Bancroft	1s. 0d.
No. 12.	Lullaby (Brahms) (2 Treble Pipes and Piano)	arr. A. M. Scott	4d.
*No. 13.	Two Classical Airs (a) Allegro (Mozart) (Treble and Tenor), (b) Passepied II. (Bach) (Trio)	arr. Elsa Boyd	4d.
No. 14.	Dimple Cheek (Quartet)	arr. Annie Z. Miller	4d.
No. 15.	Seek-Sorrow (Quartet)	Eva Pain	6d.
*No. 16.	Two Duets—(a) Bourree, (b) The Tarn (for Treble and Alto)	Eva Pain	6d.
No. 17.	Evening Song (for Treble and Piano)	Richard Hall	6d.
No. 18.	Gioite al Canto Mio (Peri) (Quartet)	arr. ,, ,,	6d.
No. 19.	Canzonetta No. 1 (Quartet)	,, ,,	6d.
No. 20.	Canzonetta No. 2 (Trio)	,, ,,	6d.
No. 21.	Morning Song (Alto and Piano)	,, ,,	4d.
No. 22.	Two Trios (a) Scottish Air (for Alto, Tenor and Bass) (b) Flibbberty Gibbety Sarah (for Treble, Tenor and Bass)	Eva Pain	6d.
No. 23.	Jig (for Treble and Piano)	Margaret Witton	4d.
No. 24.	Betty's Break (Trio for Treble, Alto and Tenor)	Denis Capes	4d.
No. 25.	Early in the Morning (Trio for 2 Tenor and 1 Bass)	,, ,,	4d.
No. 26.	Susan (An Air with words for "Group" playing and alternate singing)	,, ,,	4d.
No. 27.	Melody for Community Playing (Treble Pipes and P.F. with Alto and Tenor, ad-lib.)	,, ,,	4d.
No. 28.	The Cuckoo Clock (Duet for Treble, Alto or Tenor Pipes)	Richard Hall	4d.
No. 29.	(a) Bourree } (Bach) (Duets for Treble and Alto Pipes) (b) Minuett }	arr. Olga Peppercorn	4d.
No. 30.	Haste O Sun (Treble and Piano)	arr. Kathleen M. Blocksidge	4d.
No. 31.	Dashing away with the Smoothing Iron (Quartet)	arr. Millicent Shepperd	4d.
No. 32.	Minuet in G (Beethoven) (Quartet)	arr. Dorothy Barnard	3d.
*No. 33.	Minuet and Trio in G Op. 17, No. 5 (Haydn) Quartet)	arr. Dorothy Barnard	3d.
No. 34.	Sailor's Song (Schumann) (Quartet)	,, ,, ,,	3d.
No. 35.	Sigh no more Ladies (Stevens) (Quartet)	,, ,,	3d.
No. 36.	Bouree-Minuet-Gigue (Trios)	Markham Lee	1s. 0d.
No. 37.	Suite Ancienne (Trio)	A. Goodchild	1s. 0d.
No. 38.	Little Rondo (Quartet) (Treble, Alto, 1st and 2nd Tenor or Bass)	Hart Hawkins	4d.
No. 39.	Reverie (A) (Quartet)	,, ,,	4d.
No. 40.	Conversation Piece, No. 1, "Andante" (Trio)	Denis Capes	6d.
No. 41.	,, ,, No. 2, "Allegretto" (Trio)	,, ,,	6d.
No. 42.	Mustard and Cress (Duet, Treble and Alto)	,, ,,	6d.
No. 43.	Whistling Song (Treble and Piano)	James Cunningham-East	6d.
No. 44.	Country Dance (Treble and Piano)	,, ,,	6d.

* For an Adjusted Pipe.

GRADED BEGINNERS' TUNES
(with piano accompaniment)
For Treble Pipes in Process of Making
By KATHLEEN M. BLOCKSIDGE
Price 3d. each.

1. The Doorkeeper, for 1 note (D).
2. Jack the Giant Killer, for 2 notes (D, E).
3. Swinging, for 3 notes (D. E. F sharp).
4. Bonnie Scotland, for 4 notes (D to G).
5. Holidays, for 5 notes (D to A).
6. Joy's Waltz, for 6 notes (D to B).
7. Caprice (Schumann), for 6 notes (D to B).
8. The Shepherd Boy, for 8 notes (D to D).

No. 1 *is a tune on One Note, No. 2 on Two Notes and so on up to the complete Scale.*

Music for the Recorder

Sonata in E Flat for Flute and Pianoforte
or
For Treble Recorder and Harpsichord
by Martin Shaw   7/6

A Bach Book for the Treble Recorder
Twenty passages from Flute parts in the Church Cantatas
arranged by Imogen Holst   1/6

For Treble Recorder
arranged (with Pianoforte accompaniment)
by Alfred Moffat   each 1/–

1. Gavotta *by Jean Christian Schickherdt*
2. Sea Chantie—*Traditional*
3. Fairy Piper (The) (Am Piobatre Sith)—*Old Highland Melody*
4. Two Old English Country Dances, from Playford's "Dancing Master"
    1. *Hampstead Heath*   2. *Temple Bar*

For Descant Recorder (or Treble Pipe)
5. Two for Leisure *by Marion Anderson*
    1. *Swing Boats*   2. *Monkey Tricks*

1/– complete

N.B.—Works for Pipes are adaptable for the Recorder or Flute.

J. B. Cramer & Co. Ltd.

Publication of Educational Works are largely used in all Schools and comprise the following subjects :—

UNISON AND TWO-PART SONGS

DESCANTS AND CAROLS

RHYTHMIC MATERIAL IN EVERY STAGE

MUSIC FOR NURSERY SCHOOLS

SONG GAMES

PERCUSSION BAND

www.ingramcontent.com/pod-product-compliance
Lightning Source LLC
Chambersburg PA
CBHW022122090426
42743CB00008B/962